A Long Wait

Story by Carmel Reilly

Illustrations by Barbara Szepesi Szucs

A Long Wait

Text: Carmel Reilly
Publishers: Tania Mazzeo and Eliza Webb
Series consultant: Amanda Sutera
  Hands on Heads Consulting
Editor: Laken Ballinger
Project editor: Annabel Smith
Designer: Jess Kelly
Project designer: Danielle Maccarone
Illustrations: Barbara Szepesi Szucs
Production controller: Renee Tome

NovaStar

Text © 2024 Cengage Learning Australia Pty Limited
Illustrations © 2024 Cengage Learning Australia Pty Limited

ISBN 978 0 17 033386 3

Cengage Learning Australia
Level 5, 80 Dorcas Street
Southbank VIC 3006 Australia
Phone: 1300 790 853
Email: aust.nelsonprimary@cengage.com

For learning solutions, visit **cengage.com.au**

Printed in China by 1010 Printing International Ltd
1 2 3 4 5 6 7 28 27 26 25 24

*Nelson acknowledges the Traditional Owners and Custodians
of the lands of all First Nations Peoples. We pay respect
to Elders past and present, and extend that respect to
all First Nations Peoples today.*

Contents

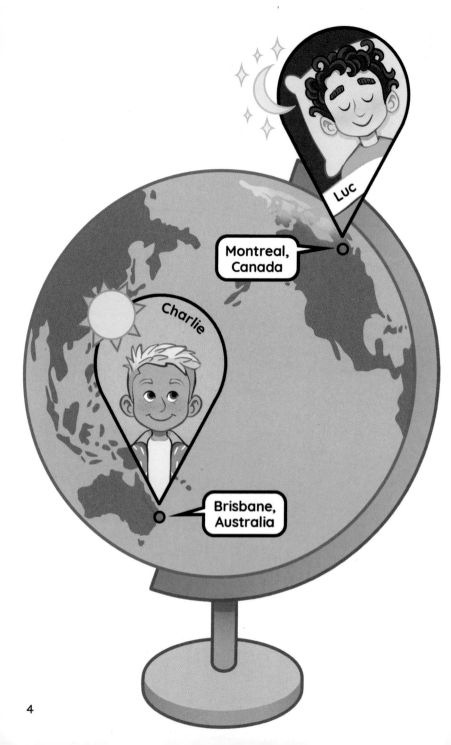

Luc

Montreal,
Canada

Charlie

Brisbane,
Australia

Chapter 1

Day in Australia, Night in Canada

Charlie turned on the family computer to find he had a message from his cousin, Luc, who lived in Canada. Luc had sent the message while Charlie was asleep. The time in Australia was fifteen hours ahead of Canada. This meant the two boys were often not online at the same time.

Hey Charlie,
Dad and I are going to our cabin
in the woods for a few days.
If it snows, we might be able to ski!
I'll message you when we arrive.
There's no computer at the cabin,
but I can use Dad's phone.

Sent: 6:30 pm
Location: Montreal, Canada

Charlie messaged Luc back right away.

Hi Luc,
It's boiling hot here. I'd love to
be in the snow instead!
Have fun, and send photos. 😆

Sent: 11:00 am
Location: Brisbane, Australia

It wasn't until the next morning that Charlie got to read Luc's reply.

Hi Charlie,
Here's Freddy running around with his ball outside the cabin. He's been going to puppy training, but he's still terrible at following commands!

It snowed this morning, so I think we'll be able to go skiing!

Sent: 2:00 pm
Location: Montreal, Canada

Charlie replied straight away.

Is it scary at the cabin, Luc?
Are there bears up there?

Mum, Lucy and I went to the beach
yesterday. Nothing scary there!

Sent: 10:05 am
Location: Brisbane, Australia

It turned out that Luc was still awake and online.

No, it's not scary here, Charlie.
The bears are hibernating now.
There are lots of cool animals
around though, even in winter.

The beach looks so nice!
I'd love to swim and sit in the sun.
Instead, I'll be hiking in the cold
with Dad tomorrow.

I'll send photos.

Going to bed now.

Sent: 8:10 pm
Location: Montreal, Canada

Chapter 2

Out Hiking

Charlie had to wait until the next day for another message from Luc.

Hey Charlie,
I'm so glad that Dad's phone gets a signal out here! Check out this photo – I saw a moose from my bedroom window this morning!

Sent: 12:45 pm
Location: Montreal, Canada

Charlie messaged back.

Wow Luc, that moose looks so cool! This is the only wildlife I've seen this morning. 😄

As usual, Rolo didn't want to move!

Mum is taking us to a wave pool today. We can rent surfboards there. It's going to be awesome!

Sent: 7:05 am
Location: Brisbane, Australia

When Charlie got back from the wave pool, he found a message from Luc.

Charlie, you won't believe this! When we came back from our hike this afternoon, Freddy suddenly raced off. We looked for him for ages, but he's disappeared! It's starting to snow again, and Dad says a snowstorm is coming tonight. We're going outside to have one last look for Freddy now.

Sent: 5:45 pm
Location: Montreal, Canada

Charlie replied, although he knew it was in the middle of the night at the cabin where Luc was in Canada.

Any news? I hope you found Freddy before the snowstorm hit.

Sent: 3:30 pm
Location: Brisbane, Australia

Chapter 3

Waiting for an Answer

That night, Charlie stayed up later than usual. He hoped Luc would get up early and reply to his message.

Hi Luc,
I thought you might be awake already and we could message each other ...

Is Freddy okay? Are you okay? I'm starting to get a bit worried.

Sent: 8:50 pm
Location: Brisbane, Australia

Mum took this photo of me at the wave pool today. It was a lot of fun. I've got to go to bed now.

Sent: 8:55 pm
Location: Brisbane, Australia

The next morning, Charlie finally had a message from Luc.

Sorry, Charlie! I tried to message you before, but the phone had no signal. The snow got heavier just as we were leaving to look for Freddy.

Then the power went out for a few hours. It's just stopped snowing, so we're going to go out and look for Freddy again. Hopefully Dad and I can find him!

Sent: 3:00 pm
Location: Montreal, Canada

Good luck!

Sent: 8:05 am
Location: Brisbane, Australia

Chapter 4

Finding Freddy

It took the whole day before Charlie heard from Luc again. A message came in just after Charlie had dinner.

> Hey Charlie, I have good news ...
> We discovered Freddy outside
> this morning!

I thought we had lost him forever.
I was really, really worried.
He was gone for two whole nights!
I have no idea where Freddy went,
although Dad thinks he might
have been sheltering in the
neighbour's barn.

Sent: 9:05 am
Location: Montreal, Canada

When Charlie started to type a reply the next morning, he realised Luc was online.

Hi Luc! You're there! How are you? You must be super relieved!

Sent: 7:07 am
Location: Brisbane, Australia

So relieved!

Sent: 3:08 pm
Location: Montreal, Canada

Is Freddy okay?

Sent: 7:09 am
Location: Brisbane, Australia

When we found him, he was shaking.
He came inside and sat by the fire.
We gave him food and water,
and soon he was back to his old self.

Sent: 3:10 pm
Location: Montreal, Canada

You mean, he's running around
and not following commands?

Sent: 7:12 am
Location: Brisbane, Australia

Sent: 3:15 pm
Location: Montreal, Canada

Here's Freddy by the fire.
I brushed his coat and put a blanket around him.

I told him to sit, but he leapt up again straight afterwards.

Sent: 3:16 pm
Location: Montreal, Canada

You'll have to take him back to puppy training when you get home!

Sent: 7:19 am
Location: Brisbane, Australia

Dad says it's the very first thing we're going to do!

Sent: 3:20 pm
Location: Montreal, Canada

I really wish we could train Rolo!

Sent: 7:23 am
Location: Brisbane, Australia

Sent: 3:24 pm
Location: Montreal, Canada